Photographs and captions by

Joe Clark, HBSS

with an essay by

Jesse Stuart

Vanderbilt University Press

Nashville · 1972

Library of Congress Cataloguing-in-Publication Data

Clark, Joe.
  Tennessee hill folk.

  1. Mountain whites (Southern States)—Pictorial
works. 2. Tennessee—Social life and customs—Pictorial
works. I. Title.
F210.C53   917.68'944   72-2880
ISBN 0-8265-1183-X

Printed in the United States of America by
Williams Printing Co., Nashville, Tennessee

ONLY ONE MILE separated Joe Clark's home in historical Cumberland Gap, Tennessee, and my Grant-Lee Hall dormitory on the Lincoln Memorial University Campus, where I lived from 1926 to 1929. Joe Clark and I had to see one another sometime on the streets of Cumberland Gap, which then had a population of approximately three hundred and remains about the same today. We students of Lincoln Memorial used to walk over to Cumberland Gap and buy supplies. And it was from Cudjo's Cave (the great cave under "The Pinnacle" of Cumberland Mountain, where Lincoln Memorial gets its water supply—a pure water, cold as ice) that I worked on the biggest and hardest work project I ever worked on at Lincoln Memorial. With a crew of Lincoln Memorial's strongest young men, we dug with picks and spades; we drilled holes by hand into the limestone rocks and blasted with dynamite and blasting powder a water line from Cumberland Gap over a foothill mountain to the little town of Harrogate and Lincoln Memorial—a line big enough to carry water for hundreds of students, faculty members, college maintenance families, and villagers.

It was then and later that Joe Clark was taking these immortal photographs of his day and time, for his own pleasure, with his little Kodak, photographs that are priceless history. His photographs have captured a time and place in the very heart of Appalachia that has practically vanished. Joe Clark, at that time, never dreamed that he was photographing for posterity; he was only taking pictures of his family, his kinfolk and friends, to go into his personal album.

Now, Joe Clark's photographs are going into a bigger album, for many people to see and to discover in his book *Tennessee Hill Folk,* a book I predict will be around for a long time to come. His book is one for libraries, schools, and people of all ages—not merely in Appalachia and Tennessee, but all over the United States. Here is the best collection of photographic history of a way of life of Joe Clark's and my people that I have ever seen. I, too, am Appalachia: all my ancestors—my mother's and father's people—are from the heart of Appalachia, and I live in Appalachia, prefer it to any place in America or the world where I have been. And this is one reason I'm happy to write this foreword about these unusual photographs, taken with a small camera by a young man who caught the lives of a stalwart people who fought for America and helped to make her great.

Many of these photographs have brought tears to my eyes. I know America has to progress. It has to change with years. We cannot sit or stand still. And I know that we in Appalachia have been slower to change than any other segment of our great country. But when I look at Joe's brother Junebug cradling wheat, I think of the times my grandfather Nathan Hylton, my father, Mick Stuart, and I have cradled wheat in the hot July and August suns on the steep mountain slopes.

I look at Joe's father, Wade Clark, taking a break from mowing fencerows, and I see my father, Mick Stuart, who mowed the right-of-way for a C&O railway section for twenty-seven years, taking time off to mow paths to the one-room schools so the women teachers wouldn't get their dresses wet in the morning dew. He was an expert with a scythe. Too bad our fathers didn't know each other.

And here is the one-room school which is not so far in the past in Appalachia. A few states still have them. But the few one-room schools left will have to go. What memories this picture will bring to millions! All my elementary work was in one, Plum Grove; and I taught my first school in one-room Lonesome Valley School. I never took a picture of it, though, or of my pupils. But Joe Clark did.

Joe Clark's great photographs here reveal the life of our people, how they worked and played. For instance, people of today who haven't danced the Figure Eight to the tune of fiddles, banjoes, and guitars have missed something in life. Joe Clark has this in an Old-fashioned Hoedown. It would be hard today to find anyone living in Joe Clark's Claiborne County, Tennessee, who hasn't hoed corn or set tobacco.

Drawing water from a well—we do it at our home every day. Our well is one hundred fifty-two years old; it has a well-sweep and a wooden bucket. The sweep is weighted on the end with old plowpoints. We have to pull the bucket down to the water. The sweep lifts it up filled with water. We have a drilled well and water piped into our house. But it is that good pure well water that is so good to drink and to use in making our coffee and tea. The well has been a part of our lives. Before we had ice, electricity, and refrigeration, we put milk and butter in buckets and lowered them down into the well water to keep them cool. Thank Joe Clark for these photographs of our early culture.

Here is a picture of a mountain funeral. The group of relatives and friends have gathered to plant forever a deceased, perhaps in a family cemetery. And so often that time comes when all relatives have died or moved away, and these cemeteries grow up in forest again; when I see these, so many in Appalachia, I think of the futility of mountain life—our people, so often planted in graves unmarked, where grass and trees will grow again. Joe Clark has caught that mysticism of mountain death in this picture.

And there isn't anything wrong with having a guitarist playing and singing at an old-time apple-peeling in preparation for making apple butter. I'm afraid these wonderful get-togethers are gone forever, where our people created their own games—and we joined them with our work. But Joe Clark records it here with a great picture. How did he ever manage to take photographs that are articles, short stories, and poems? He is unconscious, perhaps, of this fact, but this is what he has done.

To see the possum up the persimmon tree! To see one in the moonlight—to climb up and lift the possum down by his tail while the baying hounds prance on the ground below. Joe Clark had to do this. He wouldn't have got this picture if he hadn't. The same thing is true of his picture of a raccoon up in a tree!

People in Joe Clark's youth in Claiborne County, Tennessee, were self-sufficient, as they were in my youth in Greenup County, Kentucky. There was no welfare then. People had to be self-sufficient and help one another. There was scarcely a farmer anywhere, one-horse or two-horse, that didn't grow his patch of sorghum cane to make his sorghum-molasses.

This, plus wild and domestic honey, was the family sweetenin'; it could be and often was substituted for sugar. Joe Clark has caught the cane mill and 'lasses-makin' in a magnificent picture here. Many, many people can identify with this one. In parts of the country other than Appalachia where the golden sorghum is grown, I wonder if people had more fun, making long-sweetenin's at the 'lasses-mill, than we had. There was a big hole dug near the end of the long flat pan where the juice was boiled. The green skimmings were dipped from the hot golden juice and thrown into the hole. This was called the "skimmin's hole." It was usually camouflaged with crushed cane stalks. And the big joke was to get a friendly visitor—and visitors always came to the cane mills in sorghum-making time—and shove him into the skimmin's hole. All work would stop and everybody would laugh! The victim of the joke came out with green skimmin's all over him. And he himself would laugh at the prank, which was all in mountain fun.

This set of photographs, yesterday or, even today, could not be complete without the moonshine still. Before prohibition, who ever heard of a mountaineer buying his whiskey? He made it. He continued to make it during prohibition, and he often had a flourishing business. There were moonshine wars, too, resulting in death for many people. After legal whiskey was brought back, mountaineers in Appalachia continued to make their whiskey. I've just read a report saying that Tennessee leads all states in the Appalachian area in production of moonshine whiskey. Joe Clark had to have this picture, for the moonshine still has been and is a vital part of our heritage.

But there were and are some of our people who called moonshine whiskey the Devil's Brew, and they fought it from start to finish. They preached sermons against it from the pulpits of the little country churches. They lectured against it on the streets. Joe Clark has a memorable picture of these "saved" people at a baptizing. How typical to see the minister standing waist-deep in the river.

Each spring, when the ice thawed and the water warmed in the Little Sandy River, we left Plum Grove Church in a wagon train of jolt wagons, surreys, buggies, express wagons, and hug-me-tights, each vehicle loaded with people of all ages, from babies nursing at their mothers' breasts to people so old and halt they had to be lifted from the wagons. Each vehicle carried a basket dinner for the people and corn for horses and mules. All day Sunday would be given to preaching, singing hymns, and shouting, while at least one hundred people would be baptized, the proceedings often requiring as many as a half-dozen ministers. Joe Clark's Claiborne County is predominantly Baptist. Our early Greenup County was predominantly Methodist. Now, all of this has changed. We still have these baptizings, but in the earlier years they were really impressive things, especially for children to see. To be baptized in a flowing river as Christ was baptized in the Jordan was the way it had to be done.

To think that Joe Clark, a young man, through some innate, unusual ability, would think to take a picture—surely a lasting one in its great simplicity—of a typically dressed mountain man in his patched overalls carrying a hickory pole to make split-bottom chairs. Who would think of this for a photograph? This could have been a white oak pole—either white oak or hickory—and it had to be without knots. It had to be carefully chosen from a forest of trees. And with the old garden fence of palings in the background! What a superb photograph this one is among the great ones here! I used to cut white oaks for my mother to bottom our chairs and to make feed baskets, which we sold for one dollar each.

How many rural farm people all over America—not merely in Appalachia, but in Pennsylvania, Mid-America, Iowa, the near and far West, the South—can identify with and agree with Joe Clark's "Barns are some of man's most beautiful architecture." His barn photograph, a chosen site flanked by two big ancient trees—no doubt well fertilized by livestocks' droppings in the barnlot—is a magnificent one. Observing this photograph, I go back into dreams of what has been here. I'll estimate at least a century of putting feed into the loft of this barn and feeding cattle, horses, mules, and cows in stalls below.

When I entered Lincoln Memorial University, one mile from Joe Clark's home in Cumberland Gap, I came directly from the blacksmith shop of the American Rolling Mills (now Armco Steel), where I had been working as a blacksmith. Wherever I went in Joe Clark's

East Tennessee, I looked for blacksmith shops and water wheels that turned grist mills to grind wheat into flour and corn into meal. I found these everywhere. His area, in his day and time, was a photographer's paradise. I wonder now if some of his photographs aren't of the things I saw there then.

For instance, there is the home where his grandfather and father were born—and they sleep in a cemetery nearby (perhaps a family cemetery). That house was a typical early house of rural Claiborne County, also of Greenup County—also of rural Appalachia. The fieldstone chimney is a giveaway to this. Even the Greeks of Ancient Thebes where Pindar lived could identify with this. I am happy that this old home will be preserved in one of these great pictures. I call these great because they are. No one else will be able to get such picture-stories of time and place again.

Since horses and mules were essential to survival in that day and time—since buggy, hug-me-tight (a hug-me-tight was a small buggy without a top and with a seat just big enough for two), express wagon (with springs), and the great old jolt wagon (no springs) that carried the heavy loads were all pulled by mules, horses, and often oxen—here Joe Clark has preserved for us with his pictures Giant Wheels! Putting the steel rim on a jolt-wagon wheel! This is a super photograph among his great ones. I am grateful that he has caught these with his small camera for his family album. These belong to the future. Now these are immortal wheels.

His capturing the home-made bull-tongue plow and the store-bought double-shovel plow! Think of this! From the time I can remember, my father made our bull-tongue plows of locust—a heavy but durable wood—with a coulter (cutter, it was often called) in the beam to cut the roots in front of the heavy, thick steel plow shaped like a bull's tongue. This was the plow pulled by horses but more often by sturdy and steady mules and by cattle to break roots in a "new ground" field—a field cleared of timber and plowed for the first time.

Not any man who ever finished college, I'm safe in saying, has ever plowed more with a bull-tongue plow than I have, with a team of well-fed sturdy mules on the steep Kentucky hills. I have written of this plow; also, my first large book of poems is titled *Man with a Bull-Tongue Plow,* which was a natural title for me. I wonder if Joe Clark was ever kicked in the ribs more than I have been, when plowing corn with a double-shovel plow. I'm happy he's given us pictures of these immortal plows in *Tennessee Hill Folk.* I think people now and in future generations should know about them. There could well be a book on plows! Farming then and now is so different in Joe Clark's Claiborne County and my Greenup County. Here on our farm we used to use two mule teams, a span of short, stocky Tennessee mules, a span of tall, lanky Missouri mules for the steep hills, and a span of horses, each weighing approximately one ton, for plowing the level bottoms between the hills.

When I see Joe Clark's photographs of women drawing water, wearing slat bonnets, I think of my mother and all of our neighborhood women who wore the same in spring, summer, and early autumn. This was their headdress, which I thought beautiful then and still do. And his picture of quilt-making is a great one. I think of my mother, who made the finest quilts; her three daughters, my sisters, still make them. I'm glad this industry still continues among our people. To make a beautiful quilt is as creative as writing a short story or writing a poem.

Joe Clark's photos of men sitting in the country store, before their homes, talking and relaxing, are excellent and appealing. More people should join them and each try to tell the best story. I wish I could have joined these men just to have listened. Here is where I have listened and got some of my best stories, stories that have gone around the world. Never underrate what is said here. I hope oral story-telling never becomes a lost art. Joe Clark has caught these men in a relaxed, happy mood. I have meditated over his photos. I'm happy I can identify with these. Thousands more will be happy that Joe Clark has captured this rural art, which has been and is a vital part of our Appalachian culture.

I cannot identify with the fifteen-cent haircut. My father spent his Sunday afternoons cutting the hair of the men and boys in our community. There was an old retired mowing machine under the shade of a white walnut (butternut) tree, where men and boys sat while he cut their hair. He cut my hair until I left home. Then I could identify with the twenty-five-cent haircut. My father was a good barber.

The photo of a fence, across a pasture field, with posts and stakes between, is a beautiful one, an intriguing one. But we would never have had this on our farm. Our posts were locust, eight feet apart, set in the ground two and a half feet? We had five strands of number one barbed wire—or woven wire below and two strands of barbed wire above—to hold sheep and hogs. Built forty years ago, these fences are still standing—all eight miles of them. But our fences wouldn't have made a photo like this one. This is the ideal one for a great photographer. One of the super photos here among these great ones is the man letting the horse, in harness, through the gate. This one is more than meets the eye. Like so many hill farmers of the Appalachian world, where animals were and are loved and protected—and because animals were essential to our people's livelihood—this man, after working his animal, is not riding him from the field to the barn. This was a tradition among us. We never rode, or very few of us ever did, animals from the field to the barn. The animal had pulled the plow; man had walked behind and guided it. The animal had worked, too, and he shouldn't be ridden. One who had followed the plow was able to walk home. I love this photo, with its white clouds in the distance and a tired farmer and his tired horse.

Note the log houses among these photographs. I read an article that said all log houses would be gone by the year 2000. I doubt this prediction. I know Joe Clark's photographs won't be gone by the year 2000. And I know they will be here when Joe Clark, their creator, is gone. I love these photos. I think they are great. I've never lived in anything but a log house. Even our present home is partly yellow poplar logs, a wood that termites cannot destroy. Other people love them, too, and all over America people are buying them, living in them. Log houses are our heritage, except in areas where trees won't grow.

Also, will you owners of this book, readers, observers, please note the character in the faces of these photographs. Wade Clark, Joe Clark's father, with his pipe in his mouth, smoking his home-grown tobacco—in a meditative mood, at peace with the world—but look what a strong face he has. I have pondered this photograph. I've studied it. I never met this man, I never shall. But, I say, here is an individual. And here is a man who sleeps very near where he was born.

Note the face of Aunt Tilda, who has seen much time pass. She has more than wrinkles in her face. She has character. She is an individual, and I'm happy Joe Clark has photographed her for posterity. She reminds me very much of Golda Meir, Premier of Israel, who, in my estimation, is a remarkable woman—also, of Mrs. Franklin D. Roosevelt, whom I knew personally and spoke with on several occasions. Although Aunt Tilda never soared to the heights of these women, she has the same character in her face. I think she could have if given the opportunity. At least hers is a great face.

I cannot find a single face among these photographed, except for children, that does not have character written all over it. Joe Clark's relatives and friends were born individuals and remained that way. This is true of the people in our land of Appalachia, which is so slow to change to modernity.

Since I graduated from Lincoln Memorial in 1929, I have revisited this area (I cannot escape it) one and two times a year when I have been in the United States. This is one of the solid parts of America. No wonder industry from the East selected East Tennessee, a part of Appalachia; the people here are a solid people, they will work, and they have good hands. They certainly do have good hands. I know them well enough to know. This is Joe Clark's country. And you have observed this through Joe Clark's photographs of his people. Now so much of that area has been changed, modernized. But you have, in these photographs, a history of an earlier time and place of these stalwart, solid-as-the-earth, good and reliable people.

Now, one last thing I hope you observe among these photographs is the beauty of Joe Clark's country. He lived, grew up in one mile of Powell's Valley, the longest valley in the world without a river. The river is underground. This is why Lincoln Memorial University had to go to Cudjo's Cave to get water. Lincoln Memorial University is in Powell's Valley. There are still in Powell's Valley some of the landmarks photographed by Joe Clark. Many are the barns and houses in this most beautiful part of America.

It has been my pleasure to be renewed in life and living by these great photographs taken of a world I so well remember. We should be grateful to Joe Clark for capturing this world with his Kodak, even by accident, for his memory album. Joe Clark might not have been conscious of what he was doing for posterity when he was taking these photographs to suit himself. But his memory album turns out to be *Tennessee Hill Folk,* a most important book that will preserve a segment of our Appalachia for centuries to come. I hope this book will sell a million copies.

JESSE STUART

Greenup, Kentucky
August 1972

A hat used to last for many years and eventually became a part of the person.

People don't farm the valleys much anymore. They are pretty much used for pasture.

Jimmy Powell brings home the bacon.

A homemade bull-tongue plow and a storebought double shovel

My brother Junebug cradling wheat

The old springhouse with its drinking gourd and butter churn was a pleasant place.

Uncle Jim Tolbert washing up for dinner. Water runs to the house by gravity from spring up the hollow.

All dressed up and goin' to meetin' on Sunday morning

Baptizing in Olde Towne Creek

The song-master

Springtime

Wade Clark. My father takes a break while mowing fencerows.

House built by my great-grandfather. My grandfather and my father were born here. All three are buried about a hundred yards to the right of the house.

An old-fashioned hoedown

Aunt Julia McCrory and Aunt Oma Wright exchanging gossip

Listening to the Lone Ranger

Typical home with garden and paling fence

Starting up the mill wheel

The cradler

Storebought threshing machine

Setting tobacco

Time out for dinner

Hoeing corn

The old wagon has served its day and is turned out to pasture.

Uncle Harve and Aunt China

Drawing water from the well

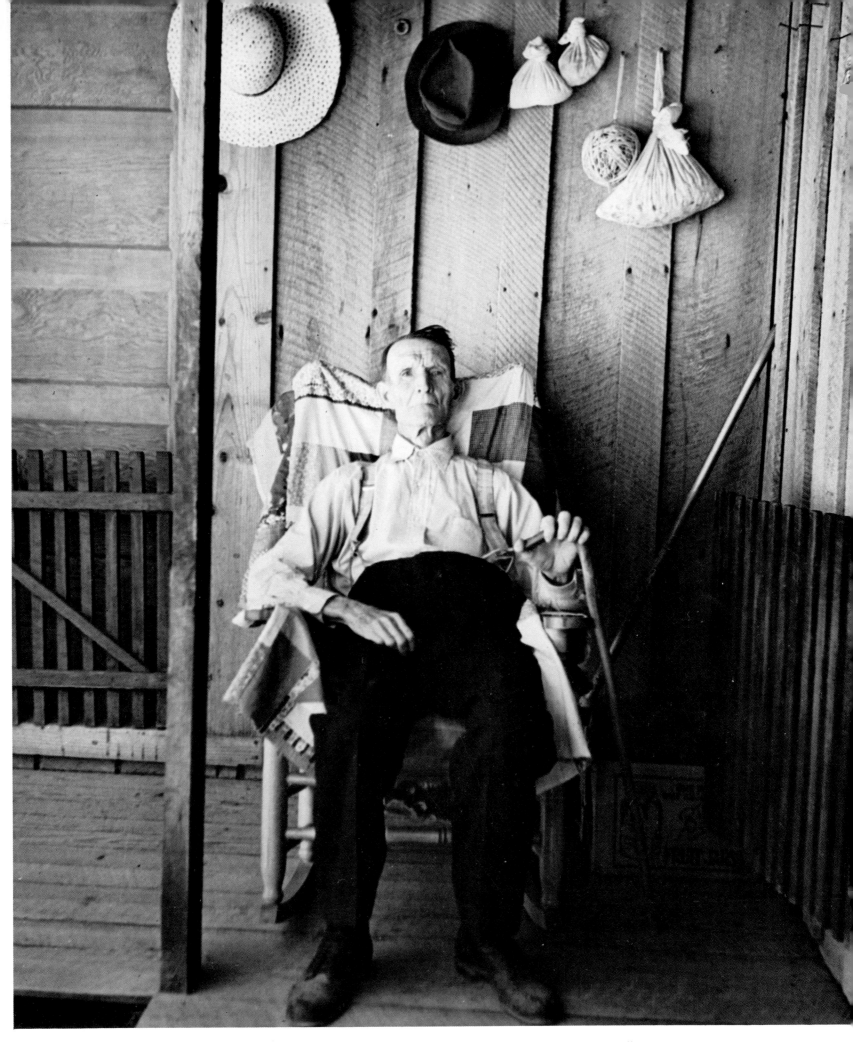

"I've seen my time but I ain't much good for work anymore."

Oldtime sawmill

The path that winds across the hill

Mountain funeral

Typical "boxed" house

Harve Smith and friendly young porkers

The listener

Walking to school

Locust Grove School

Readin' and 'ritin' and 'rithmetic

When a boy is getting his book learnin', his best friend must wait outside.

The one-room school with recitation bench

Doing homework by the kitchen stove

Doing homework by the coal-oil lamp

Rolling his own

Possum up a persimmon tree. Harry England and Otto Walker are about to shake Mr. Possum out.

A good coon hide used to bring as much as two dollars.

Barns are some of man's most beautiful architecture.

The ole swimmin' hole

Aunt Tilda

There is nothing so wonderful as a grandmother.

Momma and Aunt Nora Treece

Aunt Nora Treece carding wool

Making a little mountain dew

Looking down the valley

Singing games

Going to the store was a treat in more ways than one.

My brother Bob and Glen Sharp at the general store.

The general store

The spit, whittle, and argue club

Shopping

The shopping center

Dal Gulley's store

The general store was a great place to relax and exchange gossip.

Dal Gulley gives my brother Junebug a haircut for 15 cents.

Supermarket casualty

People of all ages loved to sit around the blacksmith shop to see and hear the goin's on.

The blacksmith shop

Uncle Alex about to tire a wagon wheel

Pappa and Bill Car mend a wagon wheel.

A berry-picker with a lard can almost filled with wild blackberries

Peeling apples for apple butter

Making sorghum

Making sorghum molasses

An oldtime apple-peelin'.

On their way to the barn

Even the gods would envy a front yard like this

Beauty is where you find it.

Sunday morning. The church in the background was built in the winter of 1795–96.

My father with a loaded pipe, home-grown tobacco, and a thoughtful mood

Typical log smokehouse

This pole is about to become a hickory-bottomed chair.

I've seen the day when possum hides brought thirty cents apiece and everybody had lots of money.

Uncle Wild and Aunt Nora Treece